OTHER HELEN EXLEY GIFTBOOKS:

Garden Lovers Quotations
The Best of Nature Quotations
Travel Notes and Quotes
Recipe Notes and Quotes

Published simultaneously in 1997 by Exley Publications Ltd in Great Britain
and Exley Publications LLC in the USA.

12 11 10 9 8 7 6 5 4 3 2 1

ISBN 1-85015-805-3

Words and pictures selected by Helen Exley.
Pictures researched by Image Select International.
Typeset by Delta, Watford.
Printed in China.

Exley Publications Ltd, 16 Chalk Hill, Watford, Herts WD1 4BN, UK.
Exley Publications LLC, 232 Madison Avenue, Suite 1206, NY 10016, USA.

IMPORTANT NOTE:
For best results we recommend that you use a fountain pen, a marker or a felt tip to fill in
this book. The pressure of a ball point pen will show through and spoil the following pages.

GARDENING
NOTES AND QUOTES

A HELEN EXLEY GIFTBOOK

EXLEY
NEW YORK • WATFORD, UK

*What was Paradise? but a Garden, an Orchard
of Trees and Herbs, full of pleasure, and nothing
there but delights.... What can your eye desire to see,
your nose to smell, your mouth to take that is not to be
had in an Orchard?*

WILLIAM LAWSON

TO DIG ONE'S OWN
SPADE INTO ONE'S
OWN EARTH! HAS
LIFE ANYTHING
BETTER TO OFFER
THAN THIS?

BEVERLEY NICHOLS

Gardens... start with months of sweat and toil, big ideas and aching joints, excitements and disappointments, successes and failures, laughter and tears. Until one fine day you realise that you're hooked and your home plot has become a part of you that you simply can't let go.

GEOFF HAMILTON
(1936-1996)

*The excitement is still there – of
sowing seeds in spring, things that
look inanimate and dead, then giving them
the right conditions and seeing them grow.
It always makes me think,
thank God there is
something in life that is certain,
that has no nastiness attached to
it. It's absolutely pure.*

CLAY JONES

ALL MY HURTS
MY GARDEN SPADE
CAN HEAL.

RALPH WALDO EMERSON
(1803-1882)

What excites me most about gardening? Knowing that whatever happens, however my fortunes twist and turn, I will be able to go out there and instantly feel better.

PATTIE BARRON

*W*hen at last I took the time to look into the heart of a
flower, it opened up a whole new world... as if a window
had been opened to let in the sun.

PRINCESS GRACE OF MONACO (1929-1982)

But a little garden, the littler the better, is your richest chance for happiness and success.

REGINALD FARRER

*A garden is the purest of human
pleasures. It is the greatest
refreshment to the spirits of man,
without which buildings and
palaces are but gross handiworks.*

FRANCIS BACON (1561-1626)

THE GREATEST GIFT
OF A GARDEN IS THE
RESTORATION OF THE
FIVE SENSES.

HANNA RION

If well managed, nothing is more beautiful than the kitchen-garden: the earliest blossoms come there: we shall in vain seek for flowering shrubs... to equal the peaches, nectarines, apricots, and plums."

WILLIAM COBBETT (1763-1835)

Far beyond hope the Spring is kind again,
Lovely beyond the longing of my eyes.

MARGARET CROPPER

With tumbled hair of swarms of bees,
And flower-robes dancing in the breeze,
With sweet, unsteady lotus-glances,
Intoxicated, Spring advances.

FROM A SANSKRIT POEM

To own a bit of ground, to scratch it with a hoe, to plant seeds and watch the renewal of life – this is the commonest delight of the race, the most satisfactory thing a man can do.

CHARLES DUDLEY WARNER
(1829-1900)

this is the garden: colors come and go,
frail azures fluttering from night's outer wing
strong silent greens serenely lingering,
absolute lights like baths of golden snow.

E.E. CUMMINGS (1894-1962)

There is nothing like a garden for making you
feel small. There you are, right in the
middle of the greatest miracle of all
— the world of growing things.

GEOFF HAMILTON (1936-1996)

A morning-glory at my window satisfies me more than the metaphysics of books.

WALT WHITMAN (1819-1892)

Gardening gives me fun and health and knowledge. It gives me laughter and colour. It gives me pictures of almost incredible beauty.

JOHN F. KENYON

For many gardeners the garden becomes a place of refuge – a private, even sacred spot where the cycle of the seasons is the only clock and time unfolds in a natural and unhurried way.

DIANA AJJAN

What other creative undertaking can produce such total submission as gardens do? They are both felicitous and predatory; they get you by the throat and do not let go. Surrender is total....

MIRABEL OSLER

In gardening, one's staunchest ally is the natural lust for life each plant has, that strong current which surges through everything that grows.

JEAN HERSEY

*I love the fact that you
can go into your garden
and concentrate on nature
and forget everything else.
Nothing seems really
important in comparison
to the joy you get from the
job you're doing.*

SUSAN HAMPSHIRE

It is good to be alone in a garden at dawn or dark so that all its shy presences may haunt you and possess you in a reverie of suspended thought.

JAMES DOUGLAS

The principal value of a private garden... is not to give the possessor vegetable and fruit (that can be better and cheaper done by the market-gardeners), but to teach him patience and philosophy; and the higher virtues — hope deferred and expectations blighted.

CHARLES DUDLEY
WARNER
(1829-1900)

One of the great things about gardening is that when the huge wave of summer does finally break, and its leaping curve of green flings into every garden a marvellous iridescent spray of petals, in colours our language hasn't caught up with yet, its joyful and indiscriminate tide lifts everyone off their feet – both proper gardeners and people like me.

PAUL JENNINGS

Mother had a touch with... flowers. She could grow them anywhere, at any time, and they seemed to live longer for her. She grew them with rough, almost slap-dash love, but her hands possessed such an understanding of their needs they seemed to turn to her like another sun.

LAURIE LEE

GARDENS ARE THEATRES;
THEY ARE THERE TO
ENCHANT, TO EXHILARATE,
TO DECEIVE AND TO
CAPTIVATE....

MIRABEL OSLER

*Like the musician, the painter,
the poet, and the rest, the true
lover of flowers is born, not
made. And he is born to
happiness in this vale of tears,
to a certain amount of the purest
joy that earth can give her
children, joy that is tranquil,
innocent, uplifting, unfailing.*

CELIA THAXTER (1835-1894)

$\mathcal{E}$ARTH LAUGHS IN FLOWERS.

RALPH WALDO EMERSON
(1803-1882)

Often I hear people say, "How do you make your plants flourish like this?" as they admire the little flower patch I cultivate in summer, or the window gardens that bloom for me in the winter; "I can never make my plants blossom like this! What is your secret?" And I answer with one word, "Love".

CELIA THAXTER (1835-1894)

I should like now to promenade around
your gardens – apple-tasting – pear-
tasting – plum-judging – apricot-nibbling –
peach-scrunching – nectarine-sucking,
and melon-carving. I have also a great feeling for
antiquated cherries full of sugar-cracks –
and a white currant-tree kept for company.

JOHN KEATS (1795-1821)

You have a bad year and you are sure the next will be better. When it isn't, you begin to realise how insignificant you are in the enormous machine of nature.

GEOFF HAMILTON (1936-1996)

I can think of few diversions more soothing, more restful to the soul, than an hour spent [watering with a can], on a warm summer evening in an old country garden with a cat in attendance. The fragrance that rises from the grateful earth is like a benison; there is a subtle, shadowy beauty in the darkening soil, a ghostly music in the soft hiss and gurgle of the water.

BEVERLEY NICHOLS

Gardens, in short, have minds of their own: or rather natures of their own. I can think of no other works of art of which this is true. Musical masterpieces, once completed, are not forever sprouting new symphonies, or great cathedrals new spires, or great sculptures new arms and legs all without so much as a by your leave to their respective creators.

LUCINDA LAMBTON

When in these fresh mornings I go into my garden before anyone is awake, I go for the time being into perfect happiness. In this hour divinely fresh and still, the fair face of every flower salutes me with a silent joy that fills me with infinite content; each gives me its color, its grace, its perfume, and enriches me with the consummation of its beauty.

CELIA THAXTER (1835-1894)

What a desolate place would be a world
without flowers! It would be a face
without a smile, a feast
without a welcome.

CLARA L. BALFOUR

A real gardener is not a man who cultivates flowers; he is a man who cultivates the soil.... If he came into the Garden of Eden he would sniff excitedly and say: "Good Lord, what humus!"

KAREL CAPEK (1890-1938)

My own ideal, when entering an unknown garden, is to be sapped of identity: I want to be taken over, to be stunned, refreshed and overwhelmed by the gardener's own voice. As long as the owner has poured their heart into it, and their ego blazes with integrity – whether poetic languor or shocking bedding plants and psychedelic blossom – I enjoy the garden for the creator's personal bravura.

MIRABEL OSLER

You can take your angers, frustrations, bewilderments to the earth, working savagely; working up a sweat and an ache and a great weariness. The work rinses out the cup of your spirit, leaves it washed and clean and ready to be freshly filled with new hope.

RACHEL PEDEN

More eloquent than the art of poets or musicians are the actions of millions of ordinary mortals who immerse themselves more and more in their gardens for the only peace they know. Only in their gardens are they taken out of themselves, beyond themselves, above themselves, in their earthly paradise.

LUCINDA LAMBTON

Yes, IN THE POOR MAN'S GARDEN GROW
FAR MORE THAN HERBS AND FLOWERS –
KIND THOUGHTS, CONTENTMENT, PEACE OF MIND,
AND JOY FOR WEARY HOURS.

MARY HOWITT

Even if something is left undone,
everyone must take time to sit still
and watch the leaves turn.

ELIZABETH LAWRENCE

Gardening is a habit of which I hope never to be cured,
one shared with an array of fascinating people who
helped me grow and bloom among my flowers.

MARTHA SMITH

*... the earth, gentle and
indulgent, ever subservient
to the wants of man,
spreads his walks with
flowers, and his table
with plenty; returns with
interest, every good
committed to her care.*

PLINY THE ELDER

I AM SPENDING
DELIGHTFUL
AFTERNOONS IN
MY GARDEN,
WATCHING
EVERYTHING
LIVING AROUND
ME. AS I GROW
OLDER, I FEEL
EVERYTHING
DEPARTING, AND I
LOVE EVERYTHING
WITH MORE
PASSION.

EMILE ZOLA
(1840-1902),
IN THE YEAR OF
HIS DEATH

I've had twelve years now, of battling, cajoling, wheedling and threatening this lump of heavy clay soil to do my bidding and produce the goods. Overall, the gods of gardens have been good to me in allowing me over the years to transform five-and-a-half acres of virgin meadow into my own little Garden of Eden.

GEOFF HAMILTON
(1936-1996)

*I*F YOU ONCE
LOVED A GARDEN
THAT LOVE WILL
STAY WITH YOU.

LOUISE DRISCOLL

PICTURE CREDITS

Exley Publications is very grateful to the following artists and organizations for permission to reproduce their pictures. Whilst all reasonable efforts have been made to clear copyright and acknowledge sources and artists, the publishers would be very happy to hear from any copyright holder not here acknowledged. Front cover images (clockwise from top left): © 1997 Omi Reyes, *Offertory Flower, 1994*, private collection; © 1997 Ellen Fradgley, *A Rose Arbour and Old Well, Venice*, The Bridgeman Art Library; Jean Louis Prevost, *Sunflowers*, The Bridgeman Art Library; © 1997 Christian R. Mirang, *Orchid Series, 1995*, private collection; © 1997 Lillian Delevoryas, *Poppy Border*, The Bridgeman Art Library. Endpapers: Vincent van Gogh, *The Poet's garden, 1888*, Archiv für Kunst. Title page: © 1997 Beatrice Parsons, *The Water Garden*, The Bridgeman Art Library. page 5: Artist unknown, *Garden Scene*, Art Resource. page 7: Konstantin Rodko, *Tending the Garden, 1908*, Superstock. page 9: © 1997 Dan Brown, *Garden With Birdbath*, Artworks. page 11: Artist unknown, *A Still Life of Asters and Hibiscus*, Fine Art Photographic Library. page 12: © 1997 Paul Riley, *The Vegetable Garden*, Chris Beetles Gallery page 14: Princess Antonia du Portugal, *Roses Roses*, Edimedia. page 17: © 1997 Paul Maze, *Jesse*, The Bridgeman Art Library. page 19: Sahir ed din Mohammed Babur, *Babur planning the Bagh-i-Wafa near Jalalabad with his architects*, Archiv für Kunst. page 21: © 1997 Llimona, *Pensativa*, Index. page 22: © 1997 Chadwick, *The Cherry Blossoms*, private collection. page 24: C.J. Robertson, *A Study of Spring Crocuses*, Fine Art Photographic Library. page 26: © 1997 A. Juergens, *Lilacs*, private collection. page 28: © 1997 Claude Strachan, *Cabbages in a Cottage Garden*, The Bridgeman Art Library. page 31: © 1997 Helen Allingham, *A Bit of Autumn Border*, The Bridgeman Art Library. page 32: Pieter Withoos, *A Still Life of Gourds and Flowers*, Fine Art Photographic Library. page 35: © 1997 Edward Wilkins Waite, *Cottage Lillies*, The Bridgeman Art Library. page 36: © 1997 von Franziska, *Garten und Park*, Archiv für Kunst. page 39: © 1997 Berthe Morisot, *La cueillette des cerises*, Giraudon/Art Resource. page 40: William Hooker, *The Trumpington Apple*, Fine Art Photographic Library. page 42/43: © 1997 Emile Claus, *La Cueillette des Choux*, Sotheby's. page 44: © 1997 Maurice Bompard, *The Poppy Garden*, The Bridgeman Art Library. page 46: Alfred Augustus Sen, *The Cabbage Patch*, Fine Art Photographic Library. page 48: Alfred de Breansky, *The Herbaceous Border*, The Bridgeman Art Library. page 51: © 1997 Istvan Mero, *Woman in a Garden*, The Bridgeman Art Gallery. page 52: © 1997 Hyacinth Manning-Carner, *Ocean Bloom*, Superstock. page 54: Jeno Karpathy, *Woman Picking Yellow Flowers*, The Bridgeman Art Library. page 56: © Timothy Easton, *Tea Under the Great Oak, 1991*, The Bridgeman Art Library. page 59: © 1997 Helen Crofton, *Delphinium Pier Point*, The Bridgeman Art Library. page 61: William Hooker, *The May Duke Cherry*, The Bridgeman Art Library. page 62: © 1997 Charles Angrand, *In the Garden, 1885*, The Bridgeman Art Library. page 64: Camille Pissaro, *Springtime Sun in the Field at Eragny, 1887*, Art Resource. page 66: George Dionysius Ehret, *Digitalis (foxglove)*, The Bridgeman Art Library. page 68: © 1997 Eliseu Meifren I. Roig, *Nature*, The Bridgeman Art Library. page 70: Claude Monet, *Flower Garden*, The Bridgeman Art Library. page 73: Vincent van Gogh, *Le Moissonneur, 1889*, private collection. page 74: © 1997 Godofredo Mendoza, *Bendera Espanol, 1982*, private collection. page 76: Redoute, *Rosa Gallica Flore Giganteo*, The Bridgeman Art Library. page 78: Camille Pissaro, *Campesina cavando*, Index. page 81: Alfred Parsons, *Hot Afternoon*, The Bridgeman Art Library. page 82: Vincent van Gogh, *Le Jardin du Poete*, Archiv für Kunst. page 84: © 1997 Patrick William Adam, *Flower Border*, The Bridgeman Art Library. page 87: Jacob Grimmer, *The Spring*, The Bridgeman Art Library. page 88: © 1997 Lillian Delevoryas, *Garden Chair*, The Bridgeman Art Library. page 91: © 1997 Timothy Easton, *Roses and Cornfield*, The Bridgeman Art Library. page 92: © 1997 Hugh L. Norris, *A Herbaceous Border*, The Bridgeman Art Library. page 94: © 1997 Timothy Easton, *Woodland Hives*, The Bridgeman Art Library. Back cover images (clockwise from left): John William Waterhouse, *The Orange Gatherers*, The Bridgeman Art Library; Jean Louis Prevost, *Sunflowers*, The Bridgeman Art Library; Dominique Hubert Rozier, *A Bouquet of Roses and Lilac*, Fine Art Photographic Library; © 1997 Omi Reyes, *Offertory Flower, 1994*, private collection; © 1997 Timothy Easton, *Shaping Up*, The Bridgeman Art Library; © 1997 Charles Edwin Flower, *Kings Manor Garden at East Hendred*, The Bridgeman Art Library.

ACKNOWLEDGEMENTS

The publishers are grateful for permission to reproduce copyright material. Whilst every effort has been made to trace copyright holders, the publishers would be pleased to hear from any not here acknowledged. LUCINDA LAMBTON: Extracts from "Are Gardens Art?" published in The Garden, May 1996. MIRABEL OSLER: Extracts from "Great expectations" published in The Garden, July 1996 and "In the eye of the Garden" published by R Dent 1993. © Mirabel Osler 1993.